NBA Champions: Washington Wizards

Forward Rick Mahorn

Guard John Wall

NBA CHAMPIONS

WASHINGTON WIZARDS

DENNY BULCAO, JR.

CREATIVE SPORTS

CREATIVE EDUCATION / CREATIVE PAPERBACKS

Guard Earl Monroe

Published by Creative Education and Creative Paperbacks
P.O. Box 227, Mankato, Minnesota 56002
Creative Education and Creative Paperbacks are imprints of
The Creative Company
www.thecreativecompany.us

Art Direction by Tom Morgan
Book production by Graham Morgan
Edited by Grace Cain

Images by Alamy Stock Photo/Christopher Szagola, 2; Associated Press/Ryan Sun, cover; Getty Images, 9; Getty Images/Afro Newspaper/Gado, 12, Bettmann, 15, Bill Baptist, 16, Dick Raphael, 19, Focus On Sport, cover, G Fiume, 10, Jess Rapfogel, 1, Nathaniel S. Butler, 5, Ned Dishman, 24, Patrick Smith, 20, The Washington Post, 3, Walter Iooss Jr., 6; Newscom/Harry E. Walker, 7; Vernon Biever/WireImage, 4

Library of Congress Cataloging-in-Publication Data

Names: Bulcao, Denny Jr. author.
Title: Washington Wizards / by Denny Bulcao Jr..
Description: Mankato, MN : Creative Education and Creative Paperbacks, [2025] | Series: Creative sports. NBA champions | Includes bibliographical references and index. | Audience: Ages 7-10 | Audience: Grades 2-3 | Summary: "Elementary-level text and dynamic sports photos highlight the NBA championship win of the Washington Wizards, plus sensational players associated with the professional basketball team such as Deni Avdija"— Provided by publisher.
Identifiers: LCCN 2024018502 (print) | LCCN 2024018503 (ebook) | ISBN 9798889892687 (library binding) | ISBN 9781682776346 (paperback) | ISBN 9798889893790 (ebook)
Subjects: LCSH: Washington Wizards (Basketball team)—Juvenile literature.
Classification: LCC GV885.52.W37 B85 2025 (print) | LCC GV885.52.W37 (ebook) | DDC 796.323/6409753—dc23
LC record available at https://lccn.loc.gov/2024018502
LC ebook record available at https://lccn.loc.gov/2024018503

Printed in China

Guard Michael Jordan

Guard Earl Monroe

CONTENTS

Home of the Wizards

Washington, D.C. is the capital of the United States. People go there to visit places such as the White House and the Washington Monument. Washington has an **arena** called Capital One Arena. A basketball team called the Wizards plays there.

Guard Bradley Beal

The Wizards play in the National Basketball Association (NBA). They are in the Southeast Division. That is part of the Eastern Conference. Two of their main **rivals** are the Cleveland Cavaliers and the Boston Celtics. All teams try to win the **NBA Finals**.

Center Wes Unseld

Naming the Wizards

This NBA team has moved a lot. They also have had many names. In 1961, they began playing as the Chicago Packers. Then they were named the Chicago Zephyrs. The team moved to Baltimore, Maryland, and became the Baltimore Bullets. They also were called the Capital Bullets and the Washington Bullets. The team has played as the Washington Wizards since 1997. The owner hoped the name would be magical for the team.

Wizards History

Tall center Walt Bellamy played for both Chicago and Baltimore. He was the NBA's Rookie of the Year in 1962. Guard Earl Monroe and center Wes Unseld helped their team reach the Finals in 1971. They lost to the Milwaukee Bucks.

The team left Baltimore in 1973. Forward Elvin Hayes pushed the Washington Bullets to the Finals three more times. In 1978, the team played against the Seattle SuperSonics in a thrilling series. They

Center Walt Bellamy

Forward/center Chris Webber

played all seven games. Hayes helped the team win their first NBA championship. The Bullets lost the Finals a year later to the same team.

Forward-center Chris Webber starred for Washington in the 1990s. Guard Gilbert Arenas helped the team return to the **playoffs** in the 2000s. High-jumping forward Antawn Jamison joined the Wizards in 2004. He led them to their best record in 26 years.

Other Wizards Stars

Smooth guard Phil Chenier helped Washington win a record 60 games during the 1974–75 season. They reached the Finals. In the 1980s, guard Jeff Malone made many tough shots. **Versatile** forward Juwan Howard was a top scorer and **rebounder** in the 1990s.

Guard Jeff Malone

Forward Kyle Kuzma

In 2017, Washington had two of the top guards in the NBA. Point guard John Wall was quick. Bradley Beal was a great three-point shooter.

The Wizards are currently led by young stars Kyle Kuzma, Jordan Poole, and Marvin Bagley III. The team is working hard to get back to the Finals.

About the Wizards

First season: 1961–62

Conference/division: Eastern Conference, Southeast Division

Team colors: navy blue, red, silver, and white

Home arena: Capital One Arena

NBA CHAMPIONSHIPS:

1978, 4 games to 3 over Seattle SuperSonics

TEAM WEBSITE:

https://www.nba.com/wizards/

Glossary

arena—a large building with seats for spectators, where sports games and entertainment events are held

NBA Finals—a series of games between two teams at the end of the playoffs; the first team to win four games is the champion

playoffs—games that the best teams play after a regular season to see who the champion will be

rebounder—a player who catches and controls the ball after a missed shot

rival—a team that plays extra hard against another team

versatile—able to do many different things well

Guard John Wall

Index